CALL OF THE WILD

The Language of Bees and Other Insects

Megan Kopp

Cavendish Square

New York

Library of Congress Cataloging-in-Publication Data

Names: Kopp, Megan, author.
Title: The language of bees and other insects / Megan Kopp.
Description: New York : Cavendish Square Publishing, [2017] | Series: Call of
the wild | Includes bibliographical references and index.
Identifiers: LCCN 2016001293 (print) | LCCN 2016004413 (ebook) |
ISBN 9781502617293 (pbk.) | ISBN 9781502617231 (library bound) |
ISBN 9781502617118 (6 pack) | ISBN 9781502617170 (ebook)
Subjects: LCSH: Insects--Communication--Juvenile literature. |
Insects--Behavior--Juvenile literature. | Animal communication--Juvenile
literature.
Classification: LCC QL496 .K68 2017 (print) | LCC QL496 (ebook) |
DDC 595.7159--dc23
LC record available at http://lccn.loc.gov/2016001293

Editorial Director: David McNamara
Editor: Kelly Spence
Copy Editor: Rebecca Rohan
Art Director: Jeffrey Talbot
Designer: Joseph Macri
Production Assistant: Karol Szymczuk
Photo Research: J8 Media

CONTENTS

Animal Communication

When people, animals, or even insects exchange information with each other, it is called communication. One individual sends a message or a **signal**. A second individual receives the message. The receiver can choose to act on the message or ignore it.

SIGHT, SOUND, AND SMELL

Social insects need to recognize other insects in their group. Communication helps insects give directions to

The beautiful pattern on a butterfly's wings communicates a visual message.

food or other **resources**. It also helps establish a **territory**, warn about danger, and find a mate. Insects do not communicate with words. Instead, they share information using sight, sound, and smell.

Visual messages can be used while on the move. These messages can often be sent without the use of extra energy

Weaver ants work together to build a nest in the branches of a tree.

and are not affected by wind. On the other hand, visual messages require a direct line of sight between the sender and receiver. They also don't work in the dark.

Some sound messages can be sent while on the move. They are fast and can travel long distances. Sound messages are effective day or night.

While sight and sound work well, smell is the most common form of communication used by insects. These are not strong smells. In fact, humans can't smell them at all. Insects share information with special chemical messages called **pheromones**.

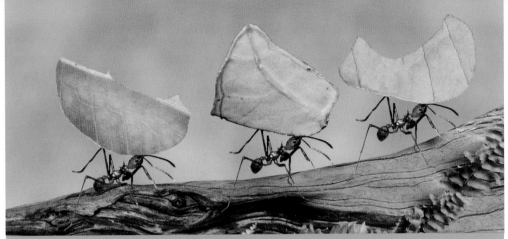

Leafcutter ants leave a trail of pheromones to mark a path between a food source and the nest.

THE SCIENCE BEHIND PHEROMONES

Pheromones are chemical messengers. They are usually found in the air, but may be left on soil or plant material. Each species of insect relies on up to one hundred different chemical messages to share information between its members. These chemicals are used to find food and mates, among other things. Pheromones travel and fade slowly. They are also effective over long distances.

This honeybee is collecting nectar from a flower called an aster.

CHAPTER ONE

Bees Dance

Communication is all about giving and receiving messages. Honeybees share information through movement. Like ballerinas, they dance to tell a story.

A WAGGLE HERE, A WAGGLE THERE

Honeybees use a unique form of body language to communicate. It is called the waggle dance. When a honeybee returns to the hive after finding food, she lands on the **honeycomb**. She moves at an angle, waggles her

abdomen, changes direction, and waggles some more. The dance follows the pattern of a figure eight.

Hives are built upright. The angle of the bee's body on the wall of the honeycomb shares information. It tells the other bees the direction of the flowers relative to the sun. Straight up means toward the sun. Down indicates away from the sun.

SHAKE IT UP!

The waggle dance also communicates distance. The bee waggles her abdomen quickly. The more she waggles, the farther away the flowers are.

Workers need to let the other bees know what kind of flower they have found. On her hunt for food, the bee collects **pollen** from the flower. The pollen has a distinct smell. Other bees watch the dance and touch the dancer with their **antennae**. This allows them to absorb the smell. They now know which flowers, how far away they are, and where the food is in relation to the sun. Several bees then fly off to collect the pollen.

Beehives are busy places. Good communication is key!

SPECIES STATS

Bees are social insects that live in hives. There are three types of honeybees: female workers, male **drones**, and the queen. All the honeybees work together for the good of the hive. These are small insects that grow up to 0.6 inches (15 millimeters) in length. Honeybees can live up to five years in the wild. A group of honeybees is called a **colony** or swarm.

A red ant uses its long antennae to sniff out trails of pheromones.

CHAPTER TWO

Ants Sniff Out Answers

A nts have eyes. They can see, but not very well. They mostly communicate using touch and smell.

FOLLOW THE SMELL

Ants work well together. They are constantly passing on silent chemical messages. Ants use pheromones to spread information. They can let each other know where to find food, such as seeds, **nectar**, or other insects. They can warn each other of possible dangers. They read scents by

Some ants act as scouts. Once they find a food source, they mark a trail back to the nest.

touching each other's antennae or heads. Ants will leave a trail of pheromones as they walk. Other ants following behind move along this trail in a row. Pheromones are also used to share which nest an ant comes from.

SOUNDING OFF

Scientists have found that some species of ants use noise to communicate. They rub their back legs over a spine running down the middle of their bodies. This makes a noise like rubbing a comb over the sharp edge of a hard surface. This noise is used as an alarm. It lets other ants know that there is trouble.

Red harvester ants live in large, underground colonies.

SPECIES STATS

Ants are common insects found all over the world. There are over eleven thousand species. Many live in tropical areas. Groups of ants are called armies or colonies. These tiny insects range from 0.08 to 1 inch (2 to 25 mm) in length. Some ants live for only a few weeks. Others live for several years.

Bush crickets are noisy, unless you spot a pair of males silently staring each other down!

CHAPTER THREE

Crickets Sing

Crickets belong to the same noisy family as grasshoppers, cicadas, and katydids. They chirp, buzz, click, and screech. These insects make noises by rubbing their body parts together.

A COMB BAND

Most crickets chirp by rubbing their wings together. When they want to make a sound, they raise their wings to a 45-degree angle. One wing has a sharp ridge called a scraper. The other wing has a series of ridges called the file. When the cricket pulls the scraper of one wing across the wrinkles of the other, it makes a noise. It sounds

THE SCIENCE BEHIND THE CRICKET THERMOMETER

There is an old tale that crickets can tell the temperature. All you need to do is count the number of chirps a cricket makes in one minute. Divide this number by four and add the number forty. This should give the approximate outside temperature in degrees Fahrenheit.

How is this possible? Like every living creature, crickets have chemical reactions taking place inside their bodies. These reactions allow their muscles to move to produce a chirping sound. Crickets are cold-blooded. They take on the temperature of their surroundings. This affects the speed at which their muscles move. The warmer the temperature, the faster the cricket chirps.

similar to running a thumb across the teeth of a comb. This movement is called **stridulation**.

A closeup look at the ridged scraper on a house cricket's wing.

Male crickets make noises, while females listen. Both male and female crickets have ears on their front legs. The ears are openings in their hard outer body. By facing one way or another, crickets can tell where the sound is coming from. Male crickets use sound to attract mates. Their **courtship** songs have loud, high notes.

SPECIES STATS

Crickets are found all around the world. There are more than 120 different species in the United States. Crickets live wherever there are plants to eat. Crickets can be more than 1 inch (25 mm) in length. They can live for up to one year.

A poisonous monarch butterfly has a distinct wing pattern and color that warn animals not to eat it!

CHAPTER FOUR

Butterflies Tell a Beautiful Story

Butterflies communicate with one another using sight, sound, and smell. Most communication is done with pheromones, but butterflies pass on messages in many unique ways.

TALKING WITHOUT A WORD

Butterfly wings are colorful and can have many different patterns. These colors and patterns carry silent messages. The colorful wings tell other butterflies which species is which. Other butterflies **mimic** non-tasty species. This fools animals that might want to eat them. Some butterflies have

21

A male cabbage white butterfly rests on a flower, waiting for a mating signal from a female.

big **eyespots** to scare away birds or other **predators**. Most of these visual signals only work in daylight.

SEEING THE LIGHT

Many butterflies can see different forms of light that are invisible to humans. Female cabbage butterflies have small patches on the upper side of their wings that reflect **ultraviolet** light. When they fly, the movement of their wings creates a flashing light. Male cabbage butterflies see the signal. They use this information to choose a mate.

DIFFERENT SPECIES, DIFFERENT MEANS OF COMMUNICATION

Scientists think that butterflies might not be as silent as they appear to be. Many species have ears on their wings, and a few communicate with sound. The male cracker butterfly makes loud noises with his wings to defend his territory and attract a mate. One

The cracker butterfly is named after the cracking noises it makes with its wings.

researcher has also discovered that blue-and-white longwings make quiet clicking sounds when they are chasing rivals out of their territory.

SPECIES STATS

Butterflies are found all around the world. Some species can have wingspans up to 4 inches (10 cm) across. Groups of these colorful insects are called by several names, including a kaleidoscope, swarm, and rabble.

In addition to his research on the waggle dance, professor Karl von Frisch also tested the ability of bees to sense color.

CHAPTER FIVE

The Buzz about Bees

Karl von Frisch (1886–1982) was a professor of **zoology** at the University of Munich in Germany. He was the first scientist to discover the meaning of the honeybee waggle dance. It took von Frisch and his students decades of research before they were sure they understood the messages behind the dance.

They did experiments using glass-walled hives and worker bees marked with paint. First, they trained the workers to find food at sources placed at known distances from the colony. Then, von Frisch and his students carefully

Honey farmers place colorful beehives near food sources.

measured both the length and angle of the dances after worker bees returned from collecting the food at these sources.

MAPPING ACTION

Some scientists are now using the honeybee dance to map the distance and location of where bees search for food each month. Honeybees fly much longer distances in the summer than they do in the spring and fall. One reason is that there are more bees in each colony to feed. The workers need to find more food. There is also competition for food from other insects. Bees are decreasing in numbers. This research will be helpful in plans to increase food sources for hives.

Bees work together to collect nectar for the survival of the entire colony.

IN THE FIELD

James Nieh is a professor of biology in San Diego. He discovered that honeybees warn others in their hive about danger with a "stop" signal. He did experiments where worker bees were attacked by other bees at a food source. The attacked bees flew back to their hive. There, a returning bee butted its head against the dancer. This was a signal to stop dancing so no other bees would fly to the dangerous spot.

Glossary

abdomen The last segment of an insect's body.

antennae A pair of thin body parts found on an insect's head that are used to sense things.

colony A group of insects, such as bees or ants, that live and work together.

courtship The behavior of male insects and other animals aimed at attracting a mate.

drones Male bees that do not collect pollen and do not have stingers.

eyespots Spots of color that resemble eyes.

honeycomb A structure made up of cells of wax built by bees to store honey and eggs.

mimic To copy something.

nectar A sugary liquid found in flowers.

pheromones Chemicals used by animals, like insects, to send messages to members of the same species.

pollen A fine, yellow dust found on flowers.

predators Animals that hunt other animals for food.

resources Usable supplies, like food or water.

signal A sound or action used to send a message or warning.

social Living in groups rather than as individuals.

stridulation The act of making sound by rubbing body parts together.

territory An area belonging to one individual or group.

ultraviolet Light with a shorter wavelength that it is invisible to the human eye.

visual Something that is seen.

zoology The scientific study of animals.

Find Out More

Books

Becker, Helaine. *The Insecto-files: Amazing Insect Science and Bug Facts You'll Never Believe*. Toronto, Canada: Maple Tress Press, 2009.

Chrustowski, Rick. *Bee Dance*. New York: Henry Holt and Co., 2015.

Murawski, Darlyne, and Nancy Honovich. *Ultimate Bugopedia: The Most Complete Bug Reference Ever*. Washington, DC: National Geographic Children's Books, 2013.

Websites

Home Science Tools: Insect Communications
www.hometrainingtools.com/a/insect-communications
Read all about how insects communicate.

National Geographic: Honey Bee Dance Moves
video.nationalgeographic.com/video/weirdest-bees-dance
Watch a video showing off a honeybee's dance moves.

Index

About the Author

Megan Kopp is a freelance writer whose passions include science, nature, and the outdoors. She is the author of close to sixty titles for young readers. She loves research and has even gone so far as volunteering to be rescued from a snow cave to get a story about training avalanche rescue dogs. Kopp lives in the foothills of the Canadian Rocky Mountains, where she spends her spare time hiking, camping, and canoeing.